something about the women

Ray Tyndale

something about the women

new & selected poems

Acknowledgements

I would like to thank Peggy Mares for this careful selection from thousands of poems, along with diplomatic suggestions for reworking or 'tidying up'. I'm often amazed at what comes out of my head and onto paper, and equally surprised to find I have a readership for my scribblings.

something about the women: new & selected poems
ISBN 978 1 76109 387 6
Copyright © text Ray Tyndale 2022

First published 2022 by
GINNINDERRA PRESS
PO Box 3461 Port Adelaide 5015
www.ginninderrapress.com.au

Contents

Introduction	7
part one: on being a girl	
femininity	11
contagion 1950	12
worksheds	13
foundations	17
the importance of being Nice	18
Stephanie	19
pale blue eyes and dreamy	20
calculus 1965	21
part two: to a new land	
farmer's wife	25
bulling	26
milking	27
burial	28
pumping diesel	29
pastorale	30
service with a smile	31
when I've got time	35
she pays her bills mate	36
shadow lines	37
women on boards	38
consider this	40
woolmark	42
fire!	44
disarmament	46
part three: portraits	
agenda	49
transgression	50

self-portrait	51
guess who's coming to dinner?	52
philanthropic conundrum	54
bush nursing	55
The Old Palace Girls Grammar 1963	56
losing it	57
photograph of island women	58
mental arithmetic	59
click	60
incongruity	61
stone circles	62
storehouse	63

part four: what's left?

provenance	67
communication	70
cover the wound	71
invalidity	72
no diagnosis	73
I could've missed all this	74
genesis	75
happy families	76
pram club	77
on Grandma's shoulder	78
good company	79
cruising	80
beatitude	81
I seduced her over dinner	82
who says?	90
anniversary	91
About the author	92

Introduction

Ray started writing poetry as a member of Friendly Street writers group before enrolling in the Adelaide University postgraduate creative writing course, completing a PhD in 2003.

From the hundreds of poems Ray has written, I offer this selection of my personal favourites, old and new. They share the lifetime experience of being a determined woman in a man's world.

Part 1 recalls childhood in England, where resistance to her mother's expectations for a ladylike future started early. Part 2 tells of the pains and pleasures of ten years of running family and farm in the Adelaide Hills. Part 3 imagines the lives of women she has never met, using a phrase from a diary, an old photograph, or a brief item in a newspaper to create their stories. Poems about her own life, about motherhood, ill health and women's love are in Part 4.

Every poem in this selection shares with us the music of Ray's poetic voice, her sympathetic insight into women's lives and her wisdom from more than seventy years of living.

Peggy Mares, Largs Bay, 2022

part one

on being a girl

femininity

there was a headless lady
at the bottom of our garden
when I was little

she had been beautiful
with flowing Grecian robes
and a crown of flowers

she did very well without her head
nasturtium and lobelia trailed
from the stump of her neck

her gown like linenfold panelling
was weatherworn   mossy and caught
at the flowers as they tumbled

she did very well without her head
looked beautiful with her brains
spilled unheeded on the ground

I learned when I was little
at the bottom of our garden
a concrete lesson in femininity

contagion 1950

halfway through the century
my childhood is half over
infectious diseases keep me in bed
with books from the public library
where chickenpox is a notifiable disease
mumps and measles also quarantine me
more often than not

when not occupied picking spots
I cut off my curls – so
carefully nurtured by Mother well-versed
in the proper looks of little girls –
no curls reappear
mother mourns for ever

I paint the dog green
with loving attention to detail
signalling creative energy
and more than a trace of devilry

the next half century
can be put to good use
as I develop towards
my full potential
in Art and Mischief

worksheds

many childhood hours spent watching
at her father's elbow
in his shed
her face raised to his
chattering
she was a talkative child
watching as he worked
learning to be the son
        he never had

a modest shed
just outside the kitchen door
not quite detached
from the womb of the house
tarpaper roof
rough timber walls
unclad and cobwebby
masculine but warm
        a safe place to be

laid out on the wooden workbench
were the parts of a carburettor
an idle fob watch
a partly made picture frame
and the saw-eroded mitre box
resin-filled wood shavings
unpaired nuts and bolts
perished rubber grommets rolled
on the busy surface *you never know*
        it might come in use

he prided himself on his skill
at dismantling with care and delicacy
no one was cruel enough
to ask that he mend or repair
a man of great charm   his delight sufficed
so the child stood at his side and she learnt
how engines work   how clocks work
how electric plugs work
how to use a brace and bit
a coping saw   a jack plane
a spokeshave and a carborundum stone
she learned to curl
the fingers of her left hand
beneath the sole of the plane
and watch the shavings crinkle
        and fall

she learned to build special jigs
to bore an angled hole
to dovetail drawers
and hollow-bevel a chisel
she was eager to please and
happy to learn   she was
        nearly as good as a son

given away early in marriage
she watched in disbelief
her young husband's clumsy attempts
to change a plug
or use a new plane   a gift
from his father-in-law
had he not learnt
these things from his father?
her carefully learned skills
were well-honed in marriage
but her sons could not learn
       from Mother
they turned their young faces
away in disgust and shouted *Mum!*
       it's not cool!

as the men
faded from her life
she dusted off her memories
and set up her own workshed
a place of pleasure
learning new skills to complement
the old and practising them
on gifts for friends
exquisitely turned boxes in
sandalwood   olive and home-grown nectarine
silky oak knife handles
soft aromatic salad bowls
of bird's eye huon
       remembering the father's delight

her life is dismantled now
but not left undone
like his fob watch
the passing of time has set her free
and in the fastness of her own shed
          she can share her father's delight

foundations

when her corsets no longer held
her public persona rigid and proper
Mother sent for the corsetiere

a little girl   I watched the tape wound
deftly around ample bosom fully clad
courteous measurement   modesty sustained

they murmured together as my mother bent
and stretched   turned and stood
maintaining dignity over this garment of control

'double laced at the back for shape and
hooks are easy down the front   new metal
stays are longer lasting   rubber-stopped for comfort

bend forward   madam   for the cup size'
such intimacy in the touch   the voice   such tact
a mutual understanding of social etiquette

I wasn't welcome at the fitting
no one but Father saw her without her corsets
Mother's tight figure upheld propriety

the importance of being Nice

can I have a bicycle for Christmas, Mumma, please?
    here is this lovely dollies' pram dear

I want to go to Antarctica, Mumma
    no dear that's a boy's adventure

I'd really like to be a civil engineer
    dear girl how about social work?

I've won a scholarship to opera school!
    no daughter of mine will go on the stage

Mumma, geology sounds fun
    too dirty dear   too mannish   not
    nice dear   not what nice girls do
    nice girls teach or nurse before

    marrying a nice man with a
    nice home and having lots of nice babies

I want to climb trees   wear trousers
cut my hair short   grow a beard
I want to get my fingers in the dirt
go bush   mend the brakes of the car
drive a truck   play cricket
I want to look a fright   hold my own
be a boy   love women
who knows   who cares?   Mumma does

Stephanie

the name called out by a child in the street
flies me to a girlhood long-leggèd friend
in that moment the heart thuds a recognition
        of first love

she was Titania to my Puck   soprano
to my alto   bowler to my fielder
between us we shredded the pride
        of the boys' cricket team

arm in arm we lolloped back from school
ten year old girls at home in a world
created by our own imaginings
        ourselves at its core

dark curly hair in unruly ringlets
tall thin and highly strung   I thought her beautiful
with the call of a child   I recognise
        Stephanie lives in my heart

pale blue eyes and dreamy

Jill broke the pattern of dark curls
even her eyelashes were blond   and the fine
down on her skin   her eyes were pale
        pale blue and dreamy

she did all the things I loved doing
rode a pushbike   climbed mountains
folk-danced   gardened   read books
        for hours on end

when we talked   her lips reddened
moistened with excitement in shared secrets
her voice gentle and mesmeric as lapping waves
        on a shallow shore

Jill married a dreamy blue-eyed boy
I was trapped by her ex-boyfriend who
removed me from the realm of women and girls
        for twenty dry years

calculus 1965

the dry scratchy world of economics
was a compromise   better than nursing
worse than engineering but acceptable
for a woman   before marriage

Her Majesty's Treasury   dark
corridors and shit-brown paint
one step up from a prison but
still at Her Pleasure

numbers   numbers   numbers
calculus   logarithms   mathematics
tight Oxford graduates (men
of course) keeping Britain afloat

the position was mine because I was
beautiful and bright and young:
the parliamentary under-secretary
predatory   his marriage splintering

the computer   long before binary
filled a basement ballroom
became my boon companion
a fitting place for a woman

logarithm tables in hand   I fed
copious statistics into this monster
which spewed miles of paper   better
answers and quicker in my head

but it gave the Oxford graduates
something to chew over   they
no doubt run banks now and still
have a girl to use the computer
I had a baby   of course

part two

to a new land

farmer's wife

the cows milked and the chooks shut up
the bread baked and the dishes done
the pickers' pay packeted and the books up-to-date
the garden watered and fresh flowers in the house
homework supervised and a square meal eaten
the tractor spares ordered and the vet assisted
at a post-mortem
on a hand-reared calf
a yearling
that's now a dead loss

no need for Serapax or Mogadon or Valium
no need for Horlicks or Milo or hot milk
the farmer's wife sleeps every night
the sleep of total exhaustion
she groans with relief
as her body unfolds
onto the mattress and
as he clambers on top of her
like the prize Poll Hereford bull
in the paddock
she is beyond caring

she is rocked to sleep already thinking
of what tomorrow brings when the pickers arrive
at five

bulling

the cow throws a startled groan
over her shoulder blade
the AI man reaches the metal probe
far into her fiery insides
rubber-gloved hand playing
across her twitching flank
to find exactly the right spot
      frozen semen is shot
sex is over for another season

I think to myself
how is his sex life   this AI man?
I can't quite look him in the eye
as I write the cheque
the cow races down the paddock
roaring for the existential bull
the AI man and I continue
      our ordinary lives

milking

head tucked into warm flank
ear pressed to ruminating stomach
hands squeezing soft skin
life suspended   breath easy
morning and night
day after day
milker and beast together

steady rasp of tongue on chaff
hot cud steams in frosty air
the cow shifts her weight
to accommodate the emptying udder
flicks at a bushfly   the long
curly hair at the tip of her tail
entangles with the milker's own

the milk sings into the pail
rhythmically hissing against tin
building up a froth that would be
the pride of any barmaid
strong slender fingers strip
first front then back quarter
the hands well oiled with warm milk

when all is done
the cow backs out of the bail
ambles off down the paddock
the milker lifts the brimful bucket

it's not always this easy

burial

in the leaden afternoon
the eucalypts genuflect
over the empty well
as the body of the young calf
delicate as in shortened life
      slips unwanted into the grave

she sighs
hand into the small of her back
as spadesful of dry earth
cover wasted vigour
      and unbalanced books

she buries the sorrows
of the drought-stricken land
while the stringybarks droop
      to nurture her grief

pumping diesel

I see commercials with
shapely women pumping iron
in the gym to develop
their abs and their pecs
all kitted out in highcut
lycra with their legs waxed
to the bikini line and
their make-up on   and I think
to myself   they could come
out here and have dust-brown
legs without need for sunlamps
and bulging muscles from pumping
diesel – fifty-eight hand pumps to
fill the station wagon to drive
the kids to school twice a
day – no need for the
bikini line either or the make-up
because no one
takes a second look

pastorale

thank goodness for breasts!
she lay down the fencing pliers
out of reach of the toddler
hoiked up her shirt and fed
her red-faced babe in the
sudden sucking silence
contemplating the satisfactory
gleam of new sheep fence

her new son's soft wisps
of red-tinged hair lifted gently
in the warm October breeze
eyes closed / his pleasure
joining hers / her carrot-topped
daughter at her feet deeply
immersed in a tumbling tower
of pebbles and mud

service with a smile

backing the ancient blue tractor
mud flying clumpish from frayed tyres
she looks over her shoulder
at a furrow of careworn farm women

the pig-woman nourishes her piglets
as tenderly as any mother
grain and skim milk   rotten apples
then cuts   chops   minces and tops up
intestines and serves   with a smile
sausages and mash and butter
to two sons and a farmer
with blood on their hands

ii

the dairywoman tugs at cows'
rubbery tits twice a day whatever
the weather in a welter of urine
dung and kicks   alone

she turns   turns at the handle
the stainless steel discs pouring
rich cream into dishes   skim
into buckets for pigs

she serves   with a smile   apple pie with
cream you can stand a spoon up in
and the farm family clamours for more
which she always has ready

iii

the tiny woman squats over acres of
vegetables   wide conical hat shading
patient eyes   she weeds out the oats
from spring onions   painstakingly

thins carrots and radishes   picks
and bundles bok choy   mazuna   spinach
serves   with a smile   hot sour soup
with herbs and bean curd noodles

to her husband   sons and
five fellow immigrants who work
for this food and the vegetables
they take home each night

iv

this woman now   on her ancient blue tractor
nods to those others in line behind her
she collects the strawberries   redolent
with sunshine   fresh picked by immigrants

throws the waste to the cows   packs
for market in the disused dairy
boils sun-sodden fruit for jam
then drives the red truck to the city

and she serves   with a wry smile
to farmer and children
sausages with mash and butter
spinach and carrots and herbs
and a large bowl of berries and cream

when I've got time

promised time and time I'll dig out that palette
gift from Auntie Flo   must be fifteen years ago
she's been dead thirteen

as I stand outside the dairy waiting for the boys
on their mud-slathered dirt bikes
bringing in the cows   I promise myself
I'll paint the way the rays of the sun
angle up over the rocky hillside
magic and unreal like some health advert
in a woman's magazine then spread
sparkling fanwise until the sun's up
and you can't look any more
even squinting and the cows are here anyway
but my heart feels like busting
with the pleasure of it

I'm walking across a late summer paddock
to shift poddies   hat on my head
star droppers in one hand   mallet in the other
long-striding through the stubble   the air thick with hoppers
above me two wedgies float circling
circling on the thermals
couldn't I just get that lazy flight above the bare hills
the crags backlit flaming by the end-of-day sunshine
the light   the colour   the movement
palette to brush   brush to paper
if I had the time

she pays her bills mate

none of the stock and station agents
like dealing with a woman
their discomfort audible
over the satellite phone
Mrs Er? put hubby on will ya?
I'm placing big orders
they want business they'll serve me
and in a hurry
when they see money
slowly they'll come to respect
grudgingly
I know what I'm doing
I know what I want
I can pay for it
and I want it now

shadow lines

the woman pauses
as the shadow lines elongate
across the winter-ravaged paddock
the sun a pale battery hen's egg
nudging the horizon
backlighting the clump of scribbly gums
pasted as an afterthought
onto the arid landscape

she pauses
hand to her eyes
as she squints to catch
the last drops of daylight
then she flings her outback voice
to the shearing sheds   to
the rocky backdrop to the homestead
calling her lightfoot children
to their tea

women on boards

they asked me to be community rep
on the Syllabus Board
for the Ag Science department
at the local campus of the university

they met in the Senate Room
around a table bigger than our milk vat
with armchairs   water jugs and
gold-framed dignitaries

Dr This and Professor That didn't ask who I was
didn't offer me a drink   didn't even look at me
while quoting figures and bottom lines
and bums on seats and Quality Assurance

I was the only woman
I'm just a dairy farmer   I was overawed
by the Senate Room   by the experts
by the men in suits   by the qualifications

until they rose to leave when I said
in a small woman's voice that carries
across the paddock to call in the cows
to call in the farmer to his tea

what is the agricultural content of your course
I said   *what are you teaching my son and his mates?*
the gold-framed dignitaries held their breath
in the icy silence of ignorance

they sat back down   they looked at me
I held their gaze and asked again
what are you teaching our farm children?
but they did not know and I came away

knowing I and other farm women
must sit on more Boards

consider this

do they ever stop themselves short
these men in suits
seconded from this department and that
secure salary and superannuation
fleet car and a wife
to iron their handkerchiefs

do they ever stop short and consider
those of us on the board
dressed in our agri-politic best
the one-Fletcher-Jones-does-all suit
court shoes killing our feet
the polite intelligent expression
hiding our dismay at their ignorance

do they ever consider
the pre-dawn goodbye kiss
four hour each way drive
in the old Ford station wagon
rust bogged to avoid defecting
sky high fuel prices
school run reorganised
breakfast a cardboard two arches
they-didn't-buy-their-beef-from-us
excuse for a hamburger

when they write policy
that has no impact on themselves
does it occur to them
having gone to the trouble
to get elected to this board
to inform ourselves of all the issues
economic   social   political
having gone to the trouble
to get here at all

does it occur to them
we might want some input
might have some bright ideas
have something useful to contribute
other than to our own
superannuation fund?

woolmark

elegance sags from cracked
walls of formal dining room
falls around sterling silver
walnut table seating twenty
threadbare Persian carpet

windows – who has time
to clean them – stare over
strangled gardens   carriage drive
cul-de-sac'd with weeds

on every peeling wall
ancestors frown from their frames
they took life seriously

squatters once held balls
tennis parties   polo matches
now the homestead
barely entertains itself

the current incumbents
fifth generation sheep farmers
still winning blue ribbons
scratch and diversify:

spinning classes to use the product
dyeing workshops for classy colours
farm holidays to feed the lambs

tours around the wilderness garden
exports   expos   expert advice
gracious catered dinners beneath the
gaze of ousted forebears

meanwhile the whole carefully
husbanded estate
falls around their ears as
buyers reach for polycotton
permanent press and cheap Asian labour

fire!

it takes only one malicious spark
the air kiln-dried off the central desert
one match   one butt   one lighter
to rip the worn fabric of farm life

no fighting this prank-engendered juggernaut
watch from the broiling dam
enfolded by old and wily cattle
as the fireball consumes years of toil

the fat young weaners barbecued on their feet
rosy berries magicked into jam   apple trees
shaped by generations of care explode grenades
hurling toffee apples into the thickened air

summer sun turns autumn red in black smoke
swear you can hear steam trains coming down the track
even the soil burns at the edge of the water
air solid ash by now   singeing hair

where's the digger aiming that flame thrower?
he's got the wrong enemy tell him
tell him to turn the damn thing off
tell him the war is over

the scorched earth policy has triumphed
here Daisy, here Bruno! the steers are
roasted before the money changed hands
sticky toffee belies the fun of the fair

when the danger's over and the stumps
smoulder less intensely   city folk
come to picnic   seeing only blackened
earth and bloated corpses to exclaim over

they don't see ruined lives   charred fences
broken pumps   punctured irrigation   they
don't see a generation of growing
before the next crop of apples

they don't hear the unshed tears
the proud unspoken cries for help   they
don't hear the bank manager refusing
a burnt farm as collateral

they don't smell the rotting carcasses
bulldozed down the old well   don't
smell the fear   the dread   the knowledge
of a hard life come to nought

disarmament

she was the atom bomb of Kenton Valley
a fury of energy and initiative and joy
of milking and child-rearing and fruit picking
and bookwork both intellectual and
businesslike with
pickers to direct   placate   tax and pay
agents to cajole   placate   be taxed and not paid much by
children to love   cosset   hustle and taxi
to school and ballet and footy and band
and a husband
to think for

on Ash Wednesday
when the bushfire came through
the bomb was detonated exploding
imploding   the energy dissipated
family fragmented
farm almost given away
health and vitality undone

now a damp squib
energy must be fought for
joy hard won and barely

she is harmless now
disarmed

part three

portraits

agenda

the male poet
driven by ego
inflated
more often than not
cannot imagine
the protagonist
as anybody
other than himself

the woman poet
peoples her words
from her wildfire imaginings
ego supplanted

just imagine
whose poem this is

transgression

I am woman
I am decisive
I choose to eat the apple

God in His wisdom
will recognise my ability
to choose for myself

I grasp the knowledge
maybe I'll share it with Adam
maybe I won't

self-portrait

after a painting of that name by Dora Chapman (1940) in the Art Gallery of South Australia

every one who comes through the gallery
stops in front of *this* woman   takes
some of her strength   still leaving
armloads for each next view
looks into her not quite straight
in-your-face eyeball stare   acknowledges
her quirky cocked eyebrow   her firm chin
the decisive clenched hand
sensible home-worn clothes
likes the full mouth   the red felt hat
sees no clutter   no tools of trade

could I portray myself in words
with steadfast courage   staring
almost straight at the reader
my lack of femininity shouting
rebellion against all norms
my list-ridden orderliness   anal
retention laid bare   all my uncertainties
is it good enough   who do I think I am?
will the reader take strength
from my words and move on
knowing more about themselves?

guess who's coming to dinner?

in the sharp sweet interval
between tea and dinner
Virginia stands sentinel at her desk
nib splattering out onto paper
her woeful difficulties with servants

the unreliability   the rudeness
the wayward bad-tempered disloyalty
unappreciative of her own generosity
and patience and restraint
who will rid me of this turbulent cook?

at this moment Nelly the cook
will hand in her own notice   *ma'am*

> *seein' as I don't give satisfaction*
> *Mrs Woolf – references, if you please*
> *and six you was havin' for dinner*
> *tonight was it, ma'am?*

dinner at eight!   no wait
my new blue dress or Clive will laugh
and where is my comb and an apron and however
did that wretched woman work this range?

she chopped and she stirred and she pulled
back the hair off her anxious lined brow
and she dabbed at the flour on her long fine nose
all the while 'trembling
>under the sense of complete failure'*

'the truth is I cannot write' she muttered
'I cannot write' *and I cannot cook*
she paused in her culinary apprenticeship and dwelled
in the kitchen gloom on the latest reviews
of *The Waves* the unkind thrusts and barbs

ignorant man! can't he see that I caught it
precisely the light and intensity just
as it should be how dare he he's wrong!
I cannot write and I cannot cook
and I cannot deal with my servants

Leonard's heart jumped when he found her at eight
lost in thought the dinner forgotten
she had left the debris of burnt pots and pans
to stand in the midst of everything
with a silver comb in her hand

* *Virginia Woolf Diaries*, Vol. 4, 15 September 1931

philanthropic conundrum

but I being poor have only my dreams
'Had I the heavens' embroider'd cloths' – W.B. Yeats

I see her in my dreams
this blank-faced textile worker
lucky to be alive
pulled out of her ruined Bangladeshi
sweat shop minus one leg
alive yes but no longer
able to feed her family

I see her in my dreams
buy my clothes from cheap stores
without checking the provenance
send my meagre micro loan
to a woman in Colombia
towards the purchase of a cow
to increase her income
but I being poor…

dreams walk a familiar path
with poverty
always hoping always

tread softly
for you tread on their lives

bush nursing

they've just got off the train at Farina
right there in the photograph
they're smiling into the sun
smart dresses covered by light
cotton overcoats held together at the waist
with ties and they're both wearing
lovely shoes and modish hats
white gloves of course
and an air of purpose
mission even

they're headed to their new job
as nursing sisters for the Inland Mission
at Innamincka in north-east South Australia
1920s maybe

in the next photo they're bottoms up
still in their smart clothes
laying matting in the sand
to get the car
        /we would call it
        an old banger/
over the Cobbler dune
infamous hazard of the Strzelecki Track

they surely must have wondered
what they'd let themselves in for

The Old Palace Girls Grammar 1963

old school friends
talk as if it was
yesterday
not sixty years ago
same vigour same valour
same spark inside in spite
of greying hair and experience
lines on the face

gossip flits between
memories and recent events
filling in the gaps
of annual letters
reassuring oneself that this
is still the same girl
and I haven't changed
a bit

losing it

Is there anything I can do?
she asks repeatedly
in a sweet old lady voice
you think she's not wanting an answer
this is not true
she wants to be busy
and has slowed down
she wants to be needed
but is not sure that she is
she wants to be loved
loving wears thin with familiarity
she is all of us as we age

photograph of island women

Museum of Island Life, Skye

the women were photographed
early in the twentieth century
on the island of St Kilda
five or six of them from memory
serious   deadly serious
perhaps never photographed before
still a little fearful
of the stealing of their souls

faces of old women   bodies of young
probably not above thirty
how many children – none in sight
maybe they were unmarried
but careworn

scarves over their heads   a wimpled effect
long dark skirts
plaids around their shoulders
hands tucked away raw with cold water washing
and on their feet nothing
all of them barefoot

on the islands today
such poverty is unimaginable

mental arithmetic

the lady in the shop behind the cathedral
a volunteer
Orkney through and through
flowery summer dress
lightweight fawn cardigan
a necklace at the high
neckline of her dress
her white hair in a wavy bun
I couldn't see her shoes
I'm sure they were sensible

the lady in the shop
tried to use the calculator
reverted to adding up my bill
piece by piece
on a sheet of paper
then totting it up
in her head bless her

click

Arkaroola, the Gammon Ranges, SA

from the ridge top
the tourist
skims the surface of the world
beaut skies   great colours
amazing views
hey darl, hold it right there!…click

over there in the view
ten thousand roos a year
are shot without denting the numbers

over there in the view
the soil blows away
by the tonne every day

out on the plain
dry creekbeds wind redgums
into white Lake Frome where
no sweat
you can walk on water

look through the shutter
see one cow per thousand acres
flyblown fat-tailed wild sheep
herds of stocky goats
see the ever hopeful prospector
the multinational pastoralist
the last elder of the Adnyamathanha
hey darl, smile!…click

incongruity

Aroona homestead ruins

strange to hear
the thrum of bike tyres
as we sat at the
top of the valley
surveying the Aroona grandeur
we could have been having
our sun over the yardarm G & Ts
sitting on the rubble remains of the wide veranda
or the once gracious stone terrace
surrounded by fruit trees

but for the appearance
of four men on mountain bikes
incongruous in the shadows
of wool-driven gentility

pony traps would have been
more the thing

stone circles

who lived in these
huge stone huts
with long banana shaped
cellars and hollow
interlinking paths?

who lived so close
close within a boundary wall
scuttled between home
and loch   loch and home
unseen by what enemy?

who lived and died
birthed and sickened
fought and fished
farmed and famished
feared and loved
like us but left no hint –
who lived here?

storehouse

carefully with a torch
I crawl into someone's
carefully constructed
three-thousand-year-old pantry

stone roof stone walls
mud floor but not awash
not damp nor musty

I could happily
store the butter even now
the eirde house
or souterrain at Culsh
a Pictish housewife's dream

part four

what's left?

provenance

Coelum, non animum, mutant, qui trans mare currunt.
They change their sky, not their soul, who rush across the sea.
– Horace, *Epistles* 1.11

it's not *these dark Satanic mills* that call to me
though emotion stirs to breakout point
at the Last Night of the Proms

nor is it commuting
on tight-packed steamy trains
stuck for hours behind frozen points

it's not that fine driving rain
saturating my T-shirt
when a rosy sunset last night promised
a modicum of sunshine surely?

friends and family screw their eyes to slits
perplexed as I admit to homesickness
a yearning for roots
severed more than fifty years now

back I go to assuage
this pointless shifty emotion
only nine weeks
but long enough to miss
all that I have in Godzown
while captivated anew
by all I've lost

dove-grey softness of light
clumps of green grass
thickening at the base of fenceposts
sunlight filtered by filigree of beech
damp leaves   moss musk
the sound of peat-brown water
gurgling over worn stones

and weather   clouds now stormy black
now fluffy white gently marbling
green and pleasant land
sunshine warmth and fecundity
blown away in a day
by a blasting Scottish gale
never the routine of reliability

the sense of continuity in the landscape
who farmed these isolated crofts?
tiny subsistence fields
spread about them like the empty
boxes of a crossword puzzle
hunkered down forever

the connections of family
unfamiliar and not comfortable
desertion of the emigrant
never entirely forgiven
bitter-sweet affection of dear friends
who know I will not stay

so much of Britain is unchanged
no cryptic clue for my nostalgia
the beaches are still pebbly
the trains create impatience
the weather is as variable
as ours is not
and friends that mattered
matter still

I don't have to live there
visit now and then
turn the screw

communication

it is always strange
to ring my sister
in cold wet Wales
and find her
reading the paper
over breakfast
while I digest
my dinner more than
ten hours later

in days gone by
the line would be
fuzzy and indistinct
with a pronounced echo
now with satellite dishes
bouncing waves it is
as if she is just
down the street
it is always strange

cover the wound

asked to write about
pain and suffering
I am confounded

I hide my pain
so many camouflages
over the decades

I have become canny at pretending
otherwise I would have been
overwhelmed

Mary Gilmore's poem
Never admit the pain
has been my unspoken mantra

or I would have cried
many times over
or died

I have worn my crown
of silence and hoped
for grace

invalidity

I never thought
of loss of health
such thoughts never
crossed my mind as I
rushed about being everything
to everybody but me

I never thought my identity
was what my body could do
until it couldn't do it
any more
and I became
in-valid

invalidity for life
is a paradox
a sentence of death
within the sugared pill of
not having to work again

striving leads to frustration
the glory
of practical physical work
leads to pain and distress
loving life
means deathly weariness
I never thought
but now I do

no diagnosis

it's all between the ears they say
although perhaps not in so many words
but the inference is there

the long-suffering expression   the longing
to put the index finger to the forehead
perhaps twist it a bit

a screw loose   a hypochondriac
one whose tests always come back negative
all between the ears

in their ego-filled world they don't see
the fragile human being
in front of them

in pain   physical or emotional pain
a mix of both maybe and sad
they see only their inability to diagnose

I could've missed all this

I could've missed all this
the heart lift of sun-speckled
water unmistakable wail of newborn babe
the new technologies   iPhones   Google
young people becoming themselves
I could have missed all this

but for the blood thinners   Ratsak
Warfarin   I could have missed all this
migraines   pain   marriage break-up
the death of friends
could have   the global warming
global financial meltdown   global
poverty   disease   pandemics
missed the bark peeling from
green and pink elephant skin
of lemon-scented gum
missed brown pigeons spreading
their wings in the dust
missed sharing the pride
of thirteenth and eightieth birthdays

I could've missed all the fleeting
moments of pleasure and pain
I could have missed but
I didn't and I'm glad

genesis

can it be fifty-five years
since I pushed and breathed
and pushed and panted this
lovely woman out of my womb?

can it be that long since
I wondered at a tiny helpless bundle
feared the fragility that is
now so full of vitality and strength?

as she matures my heart lightens
now I really appreciate
the magic of birth and notice
a subtle shift in responsibility

happy families

the babe lies in his pusher
hat on   thumb in
blanket up   snug as

big brother scowls
changes the subject
raises any objection
gets on with life
which is Very Interesting

mother bursts with pride
made soft with mother love
but still with that
nobody-else-has-done-it
quite-as-well-as-me
look to her

pram club

as the family enlarges
so does the circle of friends:
women re-enter her life

husbands dismissed early
in conversation   talk is first
of child development but soon

intimacy encourages
the airing of dreams and hopes
put on hold

the company of woman
lifts her mind from the routine
of soft-boiled eggs with soldiers

on Grandma's shoulder

I'm blest
with the sort of well-padded chest
that sends small babies
off to sleep

up and down the passage
bundle over my shoulder
soft skull nuzzly   baby smell
too good for words

stop the movement
and the tiny spine arches in complaint
knees crimp up   mouth opens
piercing newborn wail

keep up the walking   keep up
the patting and the hot little body
sweating into my neck will soon
sag and relax   arms dangling
she slumps into blessed sleep

good company

'there's something about
the women in our lives'*
absolute comfort and honesty
talk about anything
no need to put on a front

humour   laughter   compassion
death   and those left behind
work   and leading a fulfilling
and ethical existence
life in all its splendour

the past both bitter
and happy   the future
hopes and dreams and
the present   the here and now
as we come together

'something about the women'

* a passing salute to Holly Near

cruising

release from marriage
was like diving naked
into a glacier lake
exhilarating but also
quite shocking

the company of women
was elusive   friends
kept allegiance with the ex
wives feared for their husbands
where were the women
I had yearned for

I had to search carefully
they had a lifetime's
experience in secrecy
breaking the code   finding
the bars   joining the clubs   tricky
heart-in-the-mouth moments
learning that the wife and
mother was Judas

starting life all over
renewed as a woman

beatitude

and she said to me in eggshell talk
she might and then she might not
I saw in that moment that my life
would proceed anyway
but never with the same élan
if she did not

and with my arms around her
as I felt her slip away she said
she would take me for granted
that   better by far than nothing
just that single thread
to attach me

and her lips were tight with fright
I might steal
that which she would give to no one
but I would never take
what was not freely given
nor ask it

and I gave her my troth
did not ask for anything
gave love for love   thought for thought
care for care   and I was given
my earthly reward
thanks be

I seduced her over dinner

i

she came laughing
I watched
as she nibbled
brown bread croutons
with pheasant paté by
Maggie Beer and I murmured
as she played with
fettucine with cream and bacon
and lightly tossed green prawns

I grilled for her
split black Genoa figs sprinkled
with demerara   garnished with
cool creamy mascarpone
we were neither of us young
I toasted her eyes
with Cockatoo Ridge champagne
and we drowned in our desire

ii I moved into her life

I stayed
one night too long
and the family
wanted to see my credentials:
was I taking advantage
would I inflict another wound

like naughty children caught
with our fingers in the cake mix
we almost
        begged permission
from our juniors   then laughing
flouted all the rules

iii I cooked up a storm

I sang to her, she played
for me straight from the music:
Brahms   Schumann   a prim
little piece of Bach   I sang
a quirky French love song and we
sat on the rug grappling
with Proust untranslated until
growing bored with temps perdus

I cooked up a storm
in the kitchen and we picnicked
beneath the spreading elm trees
on baguettes stuffed à la Provençale
and a tarte of thinly sliced apple
dribbled with apricot jam and yellow cream
from Jersey cows grazing
rich Kangaroo Island pastures
we became more compatible
with every shared meal

iv is this safe sex?

As I licked away
the sweet ripe mango
with its salty sauce
and as she spread Hudson's
Chocolate Rock ice cream as
an encore there were no
anxious moments

maybe we should have considered
disease or violence or
incompatibility or outraged
daughters-in-law   maybe
we should have had latex
instead of trust   would such
considerations have affected
our consuming passion?

v one hundred years of cooking experience

I had cooked for years
and so had she but
never before had so much love
been ladled into the bouillabaisse
so much care into the fegato
alla Veneziana   so much
attention to detail in such
ordinary things as mash and
cauliflower cheese and rice pudding

feeding the five thousand had been
a matter of habit
         unfed by desire

vi a pigeon pair

I was the answer
to her mid-life crisis
and she to mine   the exes
would find someone younger
to dish up the same old meals
on someone else's
wedding present dinner service
while she and I
could marry our talents
in the culinary department
with the coriander and the basil
and the raspberry coulis

no need for unkeepable promises
as we peeled back the artichokes
sucking the lemon and butter from
fleshy leaves with our teeth
wrapping our tongues around the
dripping hearts   little
moans of pleasure
we had unfettered licence
to live and love and eat

vii the new cookbook for longevity

after menopause a litany
begins of cholesterol and
blood pressure and rotting teeth
of gout and lumbago
and oesophagal spasm   I am
prey to all of these and so is she
we lie and comfort one another
and plot the breaking of new rules

saltless vegetables with cumin   with
ginger or many cloves of garlic
caffeine-less drinks with verbena
and geranium and sweet lemon balm
sugarless cakes with almonds   dates
and orange rind   dusted with cinnamon
olive oil instead of butter
sheeps' milk yogurt instead of cream
ricotta instead of brie
a wine-bottling with friends fills
the cellar with ruby-rich blood to be sipped
not sucked   drop by precious drop

the feast goes on forever

viii finger food for frailty

she seduces me now
with Caesar salad   into my
mouth she dribbles the
lemon-soused croutons amid
anchovy-laden crisp cos lettuce
she wipes her fingers sensuously
up my chin and I drool for her
we share the crumbs of
soy and linseed bread scraped around
the bowl   last special morsels

such lucky women   she murmurs
as I tease her
with lemon sago pudding   she
wraps her tongue about the spoon
we pour on more and more
thick coconut milk
old desire curls and flames

who says?

as my hand gentles down your arm
clasps your thin wrist
rests on your knee as I drive
moment of intimacy out of nowhere
who says older women have no passion?

as you tip your head back
slowly dribble in the French bean
soused in rocket and basil pesto
I want my tongue to follow
our feet touch under the table
waitress smirks
who says older women have
no passion?

the throbbing samba rhythms
of Friday night TV
demand a prance around the living room
hips bump and wiggle
laughing   we win our own round
flop out of breath
who says older women?

hand in the hair
soft facial skin
short round nails
scent on the hand
unhurried lips
who says?

anniversary

set the scene well
and we can both
conjure up the magic
of that first evening together
thirty years ago
still at our fingertips
we remember what we ate
and how we put it in
our trembling mouths
trembling with the wish to kiss

what we talked about even
though heaven knows our minds
were not on conversation
even down to exact sentences
now shared secrets down the years
every sense heightened in seduction

she seduces me now
with ageing beauty and the ability
to quote passages of poetry
learnt in girlhood when I wish
I had known her forever

About the author

Ray Tyndale came to South Australia from England in 1970. Past lives have seen her run a farm, bring up a family, direct an acapella group, and work variously as cook, brickie, truckie, accountant, economist, gardener, psychologist and even as a Tupperware saleswoman. All of this rich life experience, and more, informs her poetry. She has enjoyed exploring the Outback, not only having hilarious and intrepid adventures but also looking more carefully into the role of women in the bush today. She has had three poetry collections and a verse novel mainstream-published, as well as numerous self-published collections. She lives with her partner and dog Jessie in beachside Adelaide.

www.ingramcontent.com/pod-product-compliance
Lightning Source LLC
Chambersburg PA
CBHW070311120526
44590CB00017B/2624